Compiled by John Foster

OXFORD

Oxford University Press, Walton Street, Oxford OX2 6DP

Oxford New York Toronto
Delhi Bombay Calcutta Madras Karachi
Kuala Lumpur Singapore Hong Kong Tokyo
Nairobi Dar es Salaam Cape Town
Melbourne Auckland Madrid

and associated companies in
Berlin Ibadan

Oxford is a trade mark of Oxford University Press

© Oxford University Press 1993
ISBN 0 19 916602 1
Printed in Hong Kong

A CIP Catalogue record for this book is available from the British
Library.

Acknowledgements
The Editor and Publisher wish to thank the following who have kindly
given permission for the use of copyright material:

Moira Andrew for Grandma's grandma © Moira Andrew 1991; Eric
Finney for Powerless © Eric Finney 1991; Jean Kenward for Night
light © Jean Kenward 1991; Wendy Larmont for Night visitor ©
Wendy Larmont 1991; Brian Moses for Power cut and Through the
dark both © Brian Moses 1991; Irene Rawnsley for Midnight visitors
and Night train both © Irene Rawnsley 1991.

Although every effort has been made to contact the owners of
copyright material, a few have been impossible to trace, but if they
contact the Publisher, correct acknowledgement will be made in
future editions.

Illustrations by
Paul Dowling
Dominic Mansell
Caroline Jayne Church
Jenny Williams

Jocelyn Wild
Meg Rutherford
Jenny Williams
Bucke

Grandma's grandma

It's great when Mum
and Dad go out and
Grandma comes to tea.
She lets us stay up
watching things we're
not supposed to see.

One night we sat
with Coke and crisps,
Dracula on the telly
when all at once
the lights went out –
I quivered like a jelly.

The whole place
came alive with spooks,
shadows in the air.
The ghostly shape
that laughed at me was
Grandma in her chair.

'*My* Grandma,' said our
Grandma, 'used a candle
to see her up to bed.'
'Dead spooky,' I thought,
'I'm very glad we've got
electric lights instead.'

Moira Andrew

2

Power cut

A dreadful storm blew up in the night,
it rattled the windows and gave me a fright.
I pulled the covers up over my head
and held on tight to my favourite ted.

Mum got up at half past three,
went downstairs and made cups of tea.
Soon after that the lights went out.
'Mum, come quick,' I heard myself shout.

'I don't like it Mum, everything's gone black,
what's happened Mum, are we under attack?'
'Don't worry,' she said. 'There'll be light again soon,
I'll bring you a candle to brighten your room.'

4

But at breakfast time there was still no power,
the house grew colder with each passing hour.
We had to have bread instead of toast,
we wouldn't be cooking our Sunday roast.

I couldn't play tapes or watch TV
there was no hot water for making tea.
When Mum opened up the freezer door,
melted ice cream dripped on the floor.

We ate our tea by candlelight,
and carried our candles to bed that night.
Dad said we'd be back to normal soon
as I fell asleep by the light of the moon.

5

Brian Moses

Powerless

'How will I get my hair dry now?
It's still all sopping wet.'

'Hard luck, it's no good asking me.
My problem's the TV set:
It's packed up right in the middle
Of my favourite quiz show.'

'There's a packet of candles somewhere.
Doesn't anybody know?'

'If this goes on much longer
It'll ruin this cake I'm baking.'

'My power drill went completely dead:
It's stuck in the hole I'm making.'

'I'm still in the dark with wet, wet hair.
How can I dry it? How?'

'Where *are* those wretched candles?
Oh, don't bother. It's back on now!'

Eric Finney

Night light

Can I have a night light?
Yes, of course you can.
I'll put it on
the landing
to beat the Bogeyman.

He doesn't like a bright light.
He doesn't like the glare.
It swallows up
the darkness
and shows he isn't there.

8

You can have a night light
burning bright and strong
to drive away
the darkness
all night long.

Jean Kenward

9

Night visitor

I'm sure that someone's watching
From the bottom of my bed.
I don't know who is hiding,
I can only see his head.

I want to put the light on
But I'm too afraid to try.
He might reach out and grab me.
I think I'm going to cry.

Oh good! Here's someone coming –
I can hear them on the stair.
My Daddy's switched my light on.
Well!'... It's only my old bear!

Wendy Larmont

Midnight visitors

Hedgehog comes snuffing
in his prickly coat,
scuffing the leaves for slugs.

Cat comes soft as a moth,
a shadow painted on the lawn
by moonlight.

Owl comes floating,
sits still as a cat on the wall,
watching, listening.

Mouse freezes under the leaves
on tiptoe paws,
quick eyes pin-bright,
hungry.

Irene Rawnsley

Through the dark

'We'll drive through the dark,' Dad said,
'And avoid the jams that way.'
So we set out well before midnight
at the start of our holiday.

Above us the big black sky
with a glimpse of a star or two.
In front of us, long weary hours
with nothing much to do.

Mum thought she spotted a fox
as we skirted the edge of a town,
I'm sure that I saw a U.F.O.
with its ray of light beaming down.

We stopped for something to eat
at a twenty-four hour café,
then hour after hour passed by
on our dark strip of motorway.

14

Till Dad said, 'It's really a shame,
you're missing a gorgeous sunrise.'
But I was too tired to notice,
I just couldn't open my eyes.

Brian Moses

15

Night train

The train
is a shiny caterpillar
in clackity boots
nosing through the blind night,
munching mile after mile
of darkness.

Irene Rawnsley